Sharing

By Janine Amos and Annabel Spenceley

Consultant Rachael Underwood

CHERRYTREE BOOKS

A CHERRYTREE BOOK

This edition first published in 2007
by Cherrytree Books, part of
The Evans Publishing Group Limited
2a Portman Mansions
Chiltern Street
London W1U 6NR

Printed in China

British Library Cataloguing in Publication Data
  Amos, Janine
    Sharing. - Rev. ed. - (Growing up)
    1. Sharing - Pictorial works - Juvenile literature
    I. Title
    302.1'4

ISBN 9781842344910

CREDITS
Editor: Louise John
Designer: D.R.ink
Photography: Gareth Boden
Production: Jenny Mulvanny

Based on the original edition of Sharing published in 1997

With thanks to: Holly Benham, Lewis Jamieson, Chaitun Bagary, Megan and Maya Sear.

Playing with Dough

Lewis is playing with all the playdough.

Holly wants to play too.

Holly grabs the dough.

Lewis yells.
How does he feel?

Louise comes to
talk to them.

"What's going on?" she asks.

"I want the dough!"
shouts Holly.

"I was using it!" screams Lewis.

"Lewis, you sound angry," says Louise.

"And, Holly, you really want
the playdough."

Holly and Lewis nod.

"I need lots of dough to make animals," says Lewis.

"I need some to make a pizza," says Holly.

Holly and Lewis both
want the dough.
What could they do?

Holly thinks hard.

"Lewis can give me some of the dough to make my pizza," she says. "He can have the rest."

Lewis thinks about it.

He gives Holly one handful of dough. Then he gives her some more.

"You've solved the problem. You are sharing the dough," says Louise.

Strawberries!

Maya has some strawberries.

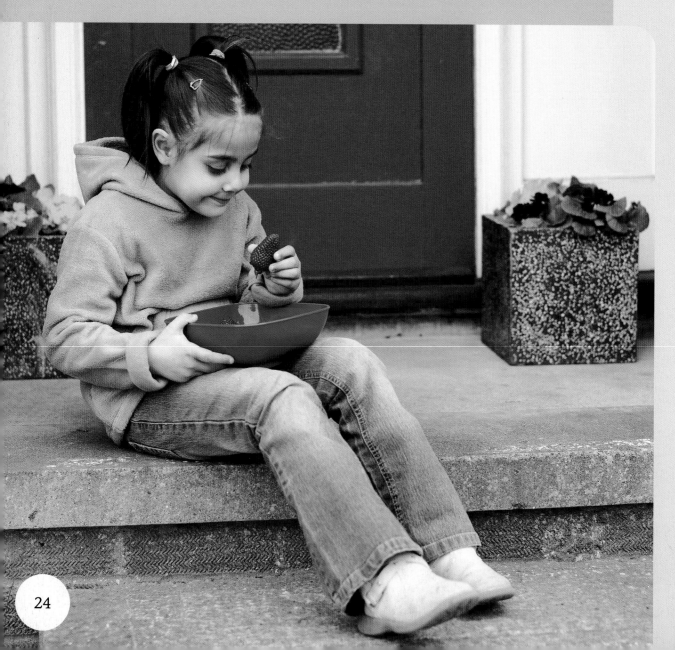

Megan comes over.
"I want some, too," she says.

"Here," says Maya.

Megan takes lots of strawberries.
"Hey!" says Maya. "That's too many!"

Megan looks at the strawberries.
"I know!" she says.

What do you think
Megan will do?

Megan gives some of the strawberries back to Maya.

Now they have half each.

Teachers' Notes

The following extension activities will assist teachers in delivering aspects of the PSHE and Citizenship Framework as well as aspects of the Healthy Schools criteria.

Specific areas supported are:

- Framework for PSHE&C 1a, 1b, 2a, 2c, 3a, 4a, 4b, 5d, 5f, 5g
- National Healthy School Criteria 1.1

Activity for *Playing with Dough*

Read the story to the children.

- Ask the children to think about all the different things we share in school.
- Scribe a list as they think of ideas.
- Ask the children to draw items from the list such as 'pencils', 'toilets', 'tables' etc to make a poster.
- Cut out and label the children's drawings to make a poster entitled 'I can share' or similar.
- As the children go through the day, ask them to identify which things from the list they have shared and to write their name on the poster beside these items.
- Encourage the children to aim to have their name on the poster next to every item if possible.
- At the end of the day remind the children of the poster and all the items on it and the names next to them. Invite everyone to give the whole class a shared round of applause for being such good sharers.

Activity for *Strawberries*

Read the story to the children.

- Have a number of cut-out paper strawberries in 3 different sizes prepared.
- Draw a 'bowl' as a circle on the board and stick 4 same sized strawberries onto it.
- Repeat the story asking 2 children from the class to stand in as the characters and share the 4 strawberries equally between them.
- This time use 6 same size strawberries in the bowl and have 3 children to share. Ask the children how it will work this time.
- Repeat this using different numbers of children and same size strawberries.
- Then move onto different sized strawberries. Stick 2 large, 2 medium and 2 small in the bowl.
- Share them between 2 children so that 1 child gets the 2 large and 1 medium, and the other child gets the 2 small and 1 medium.
- Ask the children if it is still fair.
- Take suggestions for making 'fair shares'.
- Repeat using a range of numbers, children and strawberries in different sizes.